ALL ABOARD AMERICA

Mount Rushmore

ABDO
Publishing Company

A Buddy Book
by
Julie Murray

VISIT US AT
www.abdopub.com

Published by Buddy Books, an imprint of ABDO Publishing Company, 4940 Viking Drive, Edina, Minnesota 55435. Copyright © 2003 by Abdo Consulting Group, Inc. International copyrights reserved in all countries. No part of this book may be reproduced in any form without written permission from the publisher.

Printed in the United States.

Edited by: Christy DeVillier
Contributing Editors: Matt Ray, Michael P. Goecke
Graphic Design: Deborah Coldiron
Image Research: Deborah Coldiron
Photographs: Eyewire Inc., Library of Congress, North Wind Picture Archives, Photodisc

Library of Congress Cataloging-in-Publication Data

Murray, Julie, 1969-
    Mount Rushmore / Julie Murray.
        p. cm. — (All aboard America)
    Includes bibliographical references and index.
    Summary: A brief introduction to the construction of the huge sculpture carved into Mt. Rushmore, South Dakota, and to the four presidents represented there: George Washington, Thomas Jefferson, Abraham Lincoln, and Theodore Roosevelt.
    ISBN 1-57765-667-9
        1. Mount Rushmore National Memorial (S.D.)—Juvenile literature. [1. Mount Rushmore National Memorial (S.D.) 2. National monuments.] I. Title.

F657.R8 M87 2002
978.3'93—dc21

                                                    2001055217

Table of Contents

Mount Rushmore

A **memorial** helps us remember important people and events. The Mount Rushmore National Memorial honors four great United States presidents:

☞ George Washington

☞ Thomas Jefferson

☞ Theodore Roosevelt

☞ Abraham Lincoln

Mount Rushmore (mownt RUSH-mor) is in South Dakota's Black Hills.

Mount Rushmore

Mount Rushmore is in the Black Hills of South Dakota. It is one of the largest sculptures in the world. Each president's face is about 60 feet (18 m) tall.

Detour

Did You Know?

Mountain goats live near Mount Rushmore.

William F. Cody's nickname was Buffalo Bill.

Doane Robinson dreamed of a giant mountain **memorial**. He pictured Buffalo Bill Cody **carved** in stone. Would a huge memorial of America's Western heroes bring people to South Dakota? Robinson hoped so. He wanted to make South Dakota famous. So, Robinson chose a famous artist to create this memorial. He chose Gutzon Borglum.

Gutzon Borglum was born on March 25, 1867. He was from Idaho. Borglum began studying art at the age of 17. He studied in California and France.

Gutzon Borglum

Over time, Gutzon Borglum became famous for his art. New York's Metropolitan Museum bought Borglum's **sculpture** of the *Mares of Diomedes*. This was the first American sculpture the Met ever bought. Today, Borglum is most famous for creating Mount Rushmore.

Borglum was happy to work on Robinson's **memorial**. But Borglum did not want to **carve** heroes of the American West. Borglum believed this giant memorial should be for the whole country. Together, Borglum and Robinson chose four presidents that stood for American **democracy**.

The building of Mount Rushmore began in 1927. Borglum hired about 400 people. Only about 137 of them worked on the mountain. Others built roads, sharpened tools, or helped out in other ways.

It took 14 years to create
Mount Rushmore.

Working on Mount Rushmore was hard. Workers climbed about 700 steps to reach the top. They used **dynamite** to blast away about 500,000 tons (453,592 t) of stone. They used **jackhammers** and other tools to **carve** each president's face. Some workers sat in swing seats to drill into the stone. Swing seats hang from cables.

Working on Mount Rushmore was full of danger. Yet, few people got hurt. And not one person died.

Building Mount Rushmore cost almost one million dollars. Most of the money came from the government.

Borglum ran out of money many times. This happened in 1928 and many times in the 1930s. Nobody could work on the **memorial** without money.

CHAPTER 6

Washington And Jefferson

George Washington's face rises above the other presidents on Mount Rushmore. George Washington was the first president of the United States. Americans call him the "Father of Our Country." The United States honored Borglum's **sculpture** of Washington on July 4, 1930.

President George Washington

President Thomas Jefferson

Thomas Jefferson wrote the Declaration of Independence. He was the third president of the United States. On August 30, 1936, America honored Borglum's **sculpture** of Jefferson.

Detour

Fun Fact:

The carving of George Washington's head on Mount Rushmore is as tall as a six-story building.

President Abraham Lincoln

Abraham Lincoln was the 16th U.S. president. He guided the United States through the Civil War. John Wilkes Booth shot and killed President Lincoln in 1865. On September 17, 1937, America honored Borglum's **sculpture** of Lincoln.

Theodore Roosevelt was the 26th president of the United States. Thanks to Roosevelt, we have the Panama Canal. America honored Borglum's **sculpture** of Roosevelt on July 2, 1939.

President Theodore Roosevelt

CHAPTER 8

Gutzon Borglum died before finishing Mount Rushmore.

Gutzon Borglum died in 1941. Borglum's son, Lincoln, took over his father's work.

Later in 1941, the United States entered World War II. There was no more money for Mount Rushmore. Lincoln Borglum could not finish the monument. Work stopped on October 31, 1941.

Gutzon Borglum made smaller sculptures as he planned Mount Rushmore. Here is one of them.

This is what Mount Rushmore looks like today.

The Mount Rushmore National **Memorial** stands as it did in 1941. Millions of people visit Mount Rushmore every year.

On July 3, 1991, President George H. W. Bush spoke at Mount Rushmore. He and many others were honoring the memorial's 50th birthday.

Important Words

carve (karv) to make by cutting.

democracy (duh-MOCK-ruh-see) a nation that gives power to its people and believes in equal rights for all.

dynamite (DY-nuh-might) used for blowing up, or exploding, things.

jackhammer (JACK-ham-mer) a tool for drilling rock.

memorial (muh-MOR-ree-ul) something that reminds people of a special person or event. A memorial can be a holiday, a park, or a sculpture.

sculpture (SKULP-cher) art formed from stone, wood, metal, or other materials.

Web Sites

Would you like to learn more about Mount Rushmore?

Please visit ABDO Publishing Company on the information superhighway to find web site links about Mount Rushmore. These links are routinely monitored and updated to provide the most current information available.

www.abdopub.com

Index